Dear Daughter
A Love Story

The Rules of a Big Boss LLC
Knightdale, NC 27545

Dedication

This book is dedicated to my daughter, Haelee P. Moone, Goddaughter, Cameron E. Pennix, and daughters throughout the world.

Haelee, God gave me the gift of a shero, best buddy, and unconditional love on the day that you were born. You are my shero because you have picked me up when I been at my lowest. But not only that, you overcame extreme traumas that I do not believe that I would have had the strength to endure. The bravery that you have displayed in overcoming your traumas and helping others overcome theirs is astounding. It makes you a shero not only to me, but to the world. You are truly the blessing that I do not deserve. I am so very proud to call myself your dad.

Cameron, you are too young to understand right now, but I know that it is hard not having your father around. I will not lie to you and promise you that it will get easier as you grow older. I understand this because my father was not present in my life either. What I can promise you is that today will make you stronger for tomorrow. I can also promise you that I will always be there for you. Haelee can attest that I will be at every recital, daddy/daughter dance, and when you marry your prince charming [way down the road of course]. All I need is a phone call or a text message and I will show up like Santa. Everyone knows that he never misses a delivery.

Daughters across the world, I of course cannot be there physically, but I will do all that I can to be there for you in Spirit. My writing this book is an attempt at doing so. I wrote it to reveal the heart of a dad. In so doing, I wanted to let not only Haelee and Cameron know that they are loved but so is each one of you. My hope is that it shifts the paradigm somewhat in black men not taking care of their children. I truly hope that you embrace this expression of love not only to my daughter and Goddaughter but to each one of you as well.

Introduction

It is often said that dad is the first man that a girl ever loves. Most young girls see their dads as superheroes. This does not fade with time because dad tends to be the first person that a daughter wants to call when trouble arises. What's more, it is often stated that all of their relationships in life are built off of the foundation of their relationships with their dads.

This leads to a series of questions:

Are dads really superheroes?

Do dads wear underwear over their pants?

Do dads wear capes?

Well, the answers to the questions are that it depends. Anyone that knows the story of Superman knows that he wears his underwear over his pants and a cape on his back. Superman receives his powers from the sun. It gives him super strength, the ability to fly, and a host of other powers. Dads are like him except we do not wear capes and our powers do not come from the sun. Our powers come from people like you, our daughters. Lex Luthor has no powers, but he is Superman's greatest enemy. Lex tries to destroy everything that he stands for and does not care who gets hurt in the process. Fathers are like Lex Luthor while dads are like Superman. Fathers contribute towards the birth of their daughters and not much else beyond that. Some even come in and out of their daughters lives with false promises. This leaves their daughters broken hearted over time. Dads on the other hand are there to wipe away tears, protect, love, and provide for their daughters no matter what. What makes them special is that they do not always contribute towards the birth of children. A dad can literally be an uncle, a much older brother, or a family friend. A man that picks up the mantle to fill in the gap where another dropped the ball is a Superman. My name is Dedrick, and this is the story of how I became a Superman (Dad).

Dear daughter,
I fell in love when I listened to your heartbeat and felt you kick for the first time. The doctor told your Mommy and I that you were a girl. A father would have been disappointed in that moment, but not me. You see I am a dad, and I always wanted a daughter. I wanted a daughter because I wanted someone that would look to me as their Superman. I told Mommy that you were going to be a Daddy's girl and she did not like that at all.

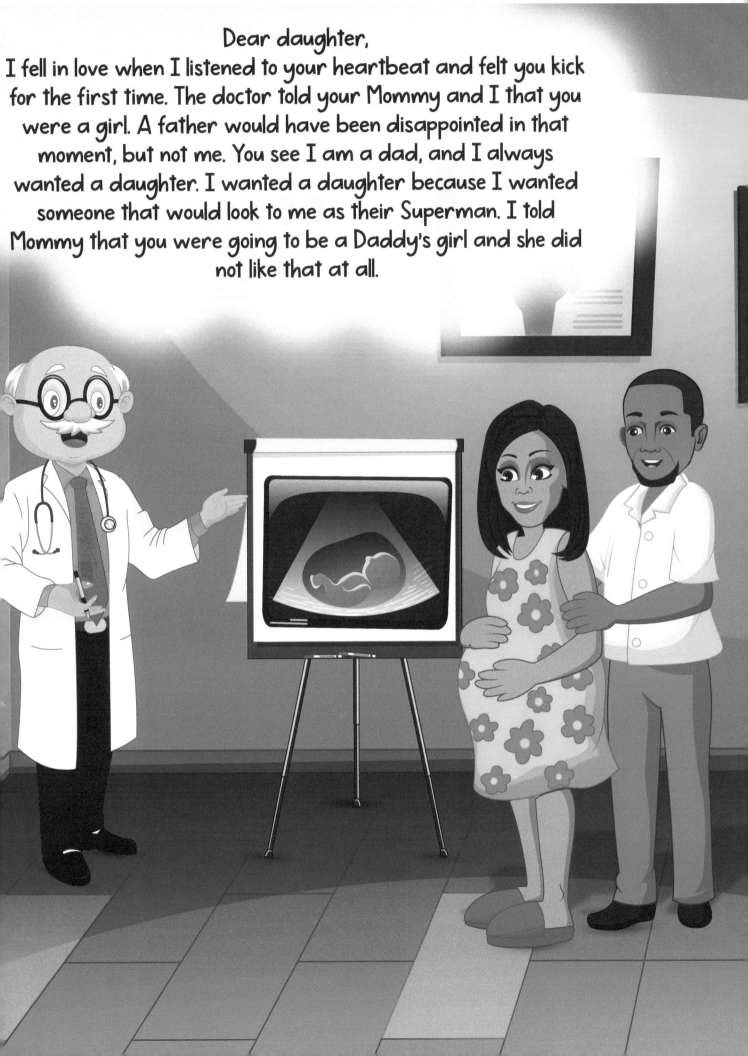

Dear daughter,

Poppy, Gran, Mommy, and I were all in the delivery room waiting for your arrival and I was a nervous wreck. Gran threatened to put me in timeout by kicking me out of the delivery room if I did not pull myself together. Her threat made me laugh and it was the medicine that I needed.

Dear daughter,

Dr. Stokes delivered you at 6:20 PM on October 18, 2007. She placed you in my arms and said congratulations. You gazed up at me momentarily as I looked back at you. You went back to sleep peacefully in my arms. Everyone was amazed that you did not cry. It was as if you knew that I was your Superman and that you were safe with me.

Dear daughter,

I gave you to your mommy so that she could see the beautiful daughter that we created as I cut your umbilical cord. She could not hold you for long though because she had severe chills. She gave you back to me a short time later to care for until she felt better. We were all so very happy.

Dear daughter,

Poppy, the nurse, and I took you to get you washed up. You kicked and screamed as she washed your hair. It was very upsetting because it was the first time that I or anyone else had heard you cry. Rage filled up inside of me because she was hurting you. I wanted to do the same thing to her, but Poppy read my mind. He told me not to do it. I began to cry as I watched you flail helplessly wanting me to save you. There was nothing that I could do about it because it was for your own good. It was for mine too because our hearts became connected during those moments where I could feel your joy and pains.

Dear daughter,

Mommy and I spent three days in the hospital with you. Everyone was amazed at your full head of curly dark brown hair, cocoa brown eyes, and caramel complexion. But most of all they were amazed that you did not cry. They said that you were a good baby, and the nurses fought over you daily.

Dear daughter,

I did not tell Mommy or anyone, but I was afraid to take you home. I was afraid because I did not know how to be a dad. I did not want to fail you, so I stepped outside to pray while you both slept. I asked God to give me the power to protect you, love you, and be whatever you needed me to be in life.

Dear daughter,

I woke up early and snuck out of the hospital on the day tha
you were supposed to come home from the hospital. You see,
wanted to give you and Mommy a special surprise. I bough
flowers and balloons for both of you and left them at the
front door so that you both would see them when we got
home. I bought you a special welcome home outfit to wear
too.

Dear daughter,

Mommy rode home with Gran and you rode home with Poppy and I when you got out of the hospital. Poppy said that we needed to dedicate you to God before we got home. We pulled over into the Safeway parking lot, lifted you up towards the sky, and prayed. I received my powers on that day in becoming a Superman.

Dear daughter,

You being a nice quiet baby did not last for long because you made up for it once we got all settled at home. You slept all day and cried all night. It was like a cruel joke had been played on us. What happened to that good baby from the hospital? The only thing that would keep you quiet was this battery-operated bouncy chair that I had bought for you. The chair had to go all night or else no one in the house would get any sleep. Mommy and I were so tired, but it was okay because we loved you and still do. But God we were so tired.

Dear daughter,
The batteries in the chair ran out a few times and there were no more to replace them. Mommy and I had to take turns dangling off the bed so that we could shake the chair while you slept. It stayed that way for several weeks until one night it just happened like magic. Mommy and I woke up in horror because we thought that you might have been kidnapped or worse. We sprang into action only to realize that you were right there in your bouncy chair sleeping quietly. We had a quiet celebration and hopped back in bed so that we could catch up on some much-needed sleep.

Dear daughter,

I promised you that I would never drop you or let you fall, and I kept my promise. You rolled out of my arms once, but I caught you in midair. But not only that you fell off the steps at the bowling alley, but you did not hurt yourself because I moved faster than a speeding bullet and caught you in midair before you hit the ground. Everyone was amazed by my superpowers.

Dear daughter,

The two of us became inseparable as you became a toddler. You and I were morning people and Mommy was not. The two of us would wake up together on Saturday mornings, eat breakfast, practice using the potty, crawling, wrestling, and watching cartoons while Mommy slept. We would have a full day of adventures by 10:00 AM. Our favorite cartoons were Little Einstein's and Elmo's World.

Dear daughter,

While you were the light of our life, Mommy and Daddy were unhappy being married to one another, so we agreed to separate and divorce. Mommy told me that she was moving to a faraway land. I was sad because I was losing my best friend and the source of my superpowers (you). I was also afraid of your not having anyone to protect you from supervillains without me there.

Dear daughter,

I took you to Build-A-Bear Workshop on the morning that Mommy and you were moving away. I wanted to give you something to protect you and remember me by. We made a Batman Bear and sprayed it with my cologne. We also recorded me saying how much I loved you and placed it in his heart so that you could hear me whenever you wanted to. You did not know it, but I was fighting back so many tears. You loved the Batman Bear.

Dear daughter,

We arrived back home, and I could not hold it in anymore. I stepped out of the car and cried like a baby because I knew that you would be leaving soon. It was like I was being served a cold dish of kryptonite because it was Father's Day Weekend. I called one of my friends and asked her for advice. She told me to wipe away my tears, enjoy the last few moments that I had with you, and to cry later. I did exactly as she said by getting back in the car and playing with you until it was time for you and Mommy to leave.

Dear daughter,

Mommy would not let me visit or talk to you for several weeks after we separated out of fear that I would turn you against her or try to take you away. I did not think that I would ever get to see you again, so I cried every day.

Dear daughter,

Our hearts were connected so you became sad too. Mommy told me that you used to ask for me daily. She wanted to make you happy, so she started letting you call me. You would always ask me where I was and when I was coming to see you. It broke my heart because I did not know the answers, but Mommy did. She eventually gave me a map to the faraway land and told me that I could come visit. I drove down that weekend and every one thereafter so you and I could spend time together.

Dear daughter,

I took you everywhere and bought you everything that your imagination could think of during my visits. It was nothing for me to surprise you with trips to Kings Dominion, Toys-R-Us, Coldstone, National Zoo, Chuck-E-Cheese, or to the mall. You did not like that Dancing Elmo that I got you for your birthday though. It was funny how you jumped back, and side eyed him when he started singing and dancing.

Dear daughter,

You began to misbehave at daycare over time. The daycare director would call Mommy so that she could speak with you about your behavior. She hoped that they could come up with a plan to get you back on track. Mommy told her that you were misbehaving because you missed me and that you felt better when you either held Batman Bear or a picture of me. The daycare director agreed to let you bring a picture of me that you could keep in your pocket and hold onto at nap time. It made you feel a little bit better.

Dear daughter,

You were still very sad, so you kept misbehaving at daycare. The daycare director asked Mommy what else she could do to help you. Mommy told her that she would have to call me because I seemed to be the only person that could make you happy. The director called me at work whenever you were misbehaving or sad. I was always happy to answer your calls even when I was in meetings. I would make you feel better by telling you how much I loved you, telling jokes, and when I was going to come see you.

Dear daughter,

I got into a serious car accident. The paramedics and the police said that I died. I remember seeing a bright golden light in darkness. The light was very far away but it was coming towards me. I could not make out what it was because it was blinding yet beautiful. I realized that it was a picture of you smiling as it got closer. I saw and felt the hand of God as He placed it on my shoulder. He said to me, "My son, I am not finished with you yet. Wake up!!" He slapped me on my back, and I woke up. I woke up to find out that my car was crushed and that the paramedics were tending to me on the side of the highway.

Dear daughter,

The doctors ran several tests to find out what was wrong with me following the accident. They said that I had some significant injuries, but that I would be okay after several weeks of physical therapy and they let me go home. One of them said that I was either incredibly lucky or blessed because I should have been severely injured or worse. I told them that I was incredibly blessed and that I had a mission in life. That mission was and is to protect, provide, raise, and love you.

Dear daughter,

We were both very sad because I was not able to come see you for several weeks due to my injuries. I pushed myself extremely hard in physical therapy so that I could heal and come see you again and soon. We were very happy on the first day that I came to see you. You jumped into my arms, gave me a big hug, and a kiss on the cheek. You said, "Daddy feel better?" and I said, "Yes ma'am my little Honeybee." It hurt my back to hold you, but it did not matter because I was happy to see you again after so long.

Dear daughter,

I had a long talk with Mommy and asked if you could live with me. She said that she would think about it, and she did, but she ultimately said no. I told her that I would see her in court, and she took me up on the challenge. I called the Justice League (church members, family, friends, and associates) and asked them to attest to the type of person and dad that I was. After I asked, 105 of them were willing to do so. Mommy realized how much I loved you and that she was facing defeat, so she decided to let you come live me so long as I made her a few promises. The promises were that I would learn to do your hair and treat you like a princess instead of a son (no more wrestling). I promised her that I would, and we hugged as we both cried.

Dear daughter,

I was the happiest man alive when Mommy agreed to let you come live with me. We did so slowly with your first spending one week, then two weeks, then three weeks, and finally a whole month with me. My superpowers were fully charged up once we got to four weeks and I became a Superman again.

Dear daughter,

I would sit on the couch while you sat between my legs so that I could try and do your hair. It would take hours for me to do it because it was long, coarse, and thick. To be honest, I did not know what I was doing but I tried. It did not matter to either one of us though because we would have fun watching Jem, She-ra, Monster High, and Barbie.

Dear daughter,

My back began to hurt from the countless hours of struggling to do your ha
I had to do research to find a salon that would do it. It was hard because
most salons did not work with children back then. I found one who did not
work with kids, but they made an exception for us. Can you imagine a
4-year-old getting their hair done in the salon every other week? Well, I ca
because I was paying the bill and still am all these years later.

Dear daughter,

It was difficult to relate to you at times because you liked Barbie and baking while I enjoyed sports and action movies. We found our common bond by blending all those things together with Barbie fashion shows and bakeoffs where the Justice League and other action figures were the judges. We had so much fun with them all.

Dear daughter,

The two of us had all types of adventures from ice skating at Canal Park, to paddle boating at Quiet Waters Park, to hanging out with celebrities at Madame Tussauds. You laughed at me whenever I fell on the ice, and I laughed at you when you fell too. We were so very petty towards each other and still are.

Dear daughter,

I never told you this, but tea parties and daddy daughter dinner dates were some of my favorite moments with you. I loved them because they made you smile and laugh. I smiled and laughed too because again our hearts are connected.

Dear daughter,

You would not go to sleep at night unless I sat by your bed after reading you a story. It made me happy to watch you drift off to sleep. I was so proud when you were able to read the stories back to me. Our favorite bedtime story was Me and My Dad by Allison Ritchie. The final page read, "My Dad is the best daddy bear there ever could be. We're together forever my daddy and me." I would always get choked up a little bit over that part and still do. I am glad that we still have that book.

Dear daughter,

Our happy life took an unfortunate turn for the worse when you met your bully. The people that were supposed to protect you from her did not. They let her take away your innocence and it broke my heart to see. I felt sad, angry, and powerless but determined throughout.
I made a lot of enemies in my fight for justice for you. I even had to go to jail for a short time. It was okay though because President Obama wrote us a letter and let us know that he was on our side.

Dear daughter,

We eventually had to move to a faraway land to keep you safe from our enemies. Having to do so was scary and it made us sad because our then home was all that we had ever known. We were okay and we survived it though because we had each other.

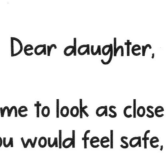

Dear daughter,

I setup our new home to look as close to our old home as possible so that you would feel safe, comfortable, and secure in our faraway land.

Dear daughter,

I shared what you had gone through with the principal and teachers at your new school in that faraway land so that they would be mindful to handle you with love and care. And they did.

Dear daughter,

I eventually lost my job because I chose to protect you by moving away. I was very sad about it because I had worked so hard for 14 years. You kept me from giving up by making me laugh, getting me to focus on what was going well, spending time with me, taking care of me when I was injured, and lending me money when I needed it to pay bills.

Dear daughter,

We continue to bond and go on various adventures in our faraway land albeit much less than we used to. You are spending more time on the phone, in the mirror, hanging out with friends, and closed off in your room. This all leads to less time with me, and it makes me a little sad.

Dear daughter,

While you are spending less time with me daily, I can appreciate the time that we do spend together whether it be watching movies, playing video games, sharing funny videos, laughing at random things, running your business, or just getting on your nerves.

Dear daughter,

I want to keep you in a bubble forever and never let you grow up. Keeping you in that bubble will protect you from heartbreak and heartache. But not only that, it protects me too. The irony is that your heart has already been broken and at a very young age. You recovered from that so I know that you can recover from anything that comes.

Dear daughter,

The strength that you shared in writing The Rules of a Big Boss: A book of self-love gave me the strength to share our story in The Unexpected Journey: Fire and Gold. You became my shero in doing it.

Dear daughter,

You deserve to see the world and live your life with all the twists and turns that it will bring. Because of that, I will have to eventually give you to someones son who I will never like in a million years. But I will do so graciously [I think] because you deserve it.

Dear daughter,

Our experiences have forged us by fire so nothing can or will come between us.

Dear Daughter,

I love you more than words can say.
Sincerely Dad

Conclusion

I wrote this story as an expression of love for my daughter. While that is the case, I want it to be a gift to all daughters. I realize that some may not be able to receive it and that is okay. Everyone will not be able to receive it because it is a very personal story between my daughter and myself. But not only that, everyone does not have a fruitful relationship with their dad or rather their father and I get that.

I personally never had a relationship with my father. As a matter of fact, I did not know who he was until I was 16 years old. My not having a relationship with him created a deep hurt within me that followed me well into adulthood. It created self-destructive behaviors and self-hate within because I did not feel loved or worthy of it. It is ironic looking back on things now because I always had a ram in the bush. I simply did not realize it. The first ram was my Uncle Tony. He served as a father figure to me throughout my adolescent years. He purchased my first bike, took me to the barbershop, taught me how to play sports, taught me how to drive, and took me to different events. Uncle Tony eventually stepped aside when Terry entered my life. He loved me enough to claim me as his son when I was a teenager and still does to this day. While that was the case, Uncle Tony was never far away in that he did not abandon me. Uncle Tony and Terry both taught me to be a man. In doing so they helped water the seeds that have allowed me to break generational curses in raising my daughter. The magic of it all is that God knew that I would need to suffer so that I could achieve the mission that He sat out over me, but while He let me suffer, He never left me alone. You see I always had a ram in the bush to serve as my dad, I simply did not realize it until much later.

My hope and my prayers are that this book allows you to see your life and your relationship with your father/dad through a different set of lenses. I pray that it serves as a sort of ram in the bush for you. Please know that I wrote it because I love you, but most of all God loves you. God is the best Dad that any of us could hope for. He is all that we truly need.

THE END

Acknowledgments

I would like to thank God first and foremost. He has kept me through all things and has been the best Dad that I could have asked for.

I would like to acknowledge and recognize my granny, Beulah M. Moone. You are my forever best friend and spiritual advisor. May you continue to Rest in Heavenly Peace. Please keep the lights on for me.

I would like to honor my mom, Wanda R. Moone. You have always been there especially when I was in danger or at my lowest.

I would like to acknowledge my dad, Terrance (Terry) G. Westry. You loved me where my father did not, and you were instrumental in my development as a man.

I would like to honor my uncle, Anthony (Tony) R. Moone. You were my very first superhero.

I would like to recognize my daughter, Haelee P. Moone for helping me write my own stories, being the source of my superpowers, and loving me without conditions.

Acknowledgments

I would like to recognize and thank Dr. Vanessa J. Raynor for being my most loving and dedicated friend. You have been there for me through my ups and downs and supported me in them no matter what.

I would like to honor Sophia L. Myles for being both a mentor and friend.

I would like to thank SherriAnita A. Pitts, Andrea N. Spence, and DeOnna S. Pierce for being my closest friends, sounding boards, adopted sisters, and keeping me laughing and encouraged throughout the years.

I would like to acknowledge Sheryl E. Smiley-Oliphant and Michaela S. Benn for giving me the inspiration to write this book.

I would like to thank Melanie P. Baltimore-Williams for giving me the gift of fatherhood.

I would like to acknowledge Gilbert E. Baltimore for accepting me into your family.

I would like to thank Janice K. Baltimore for not putting me in time out.

I unfortunately do not have enough space to acknowledge everyone. But do know that you are loved, appreciated, and valued.

About the Author

Dedrick is a philanthropist, international motivational speaker, podcast co-host, and single father. He loves to see others be their best selves, so his life's mission is to create a positive and fun impact wherever he is allowed. His hobbies include spending time with Haelee, writing, working out, designing products, marketing, vision boarding, reading, and co-hosting TalkTruth Series. TalkTruth Series gives authors and entrepreneurs a platform to elevate their brand through the sharing of their personal testimonies. Dedrick has been featured on Spectrum I News, ABC II News, WRAL News, and podcasts across the globe. He is a member of the Black Caucus of American Library Association (BCALA), Independent Book Publishers Association (IBPA), Alliance of Independent Authors (ALLi), and Literacy Nation. He is also a graduate of North Carolina A&T State University.

Contact the Author

You can connect or contact me via social media or the web. Details are provided below. I hope to hear from you.

 https://www.thebookofselflove.com

 @The Rules of a Big Boss

 @DMoone78

 @DMoone78

 @DMoone78

Don't Miss Out

Go to the link below and you can sign up to receive emails whenever Dedrick L. Moone publishes a new book. There is no obligation or commitment in signing up.

https://books2read.com/r/B-A-BSWO-WSJSB

CPSIA information can be obtained
at www.ICGtesting.com
Printed in the USA
BVHW021343140222
628968BV00006B/283